Broken Wing Butterfly

Catherine Ewing-Booker

C.U.P.
Creative Unity Publishing

Broken Wing Butterfly

ISBN 978-1-949402-04-9

Cover Design: Donna Osborn Clark at CreationsByDonna@gmail.com

Layout and Interior Design: www.CreationByDonna.com

Editing: Timothy G. Green at Inkaissance: inkaissance@gmail.com

Published by: Creative Unity Publishing
                    www.creativeunitypublishing.net

Dedication

This book is dedicated to my Lord and savior Jesus Christ
who mended my broken wing to fly again.

For those who have been hurt or wounded I dedicate this book to
you. As a child I've experienced hurt and pain, but thankfully in my
pain God still had and has a plan. If you have experienced pain and
may be suffering in silence, this book will lead you to hope and to your
purpose. My book Broken Wing Butterfly is a series of poems on how
to help navigate your emotions and how to triumph. The broken wing
represents the struggle that we have been in, but it's also a story of
resiliency because your wings will be mended to fly again

Acknowledgments

To my family, mentors and friends thank you for believing in me.

.

Foreword

By Jarell A. Ruth

When I think of my friend, Catherine Ewing-Booker. The thoughts take me back to my freshman year in college. I felt out of place and had already started to believe that college just wasn't for me. Cat approached the table where I was sitting, offering kind words and friendship. After our brief conversation, I thought to myself, maybe I can try one more day. I wanted to share this experience with the readers to highlight Cat's God given ability to heal thru words and intentions. Throughout the years, Cat continued to be there for me and offer me a fresh perspective of the issues we all face. I'm sure Cat has helped all of us in some way and that's why we've picked up her new book (Cat is the go to for fresh inspiration). Broken Wing Butterfly is a collection of pieces that continues to uplift and motivate. In a world that is currently lacking love and acceptance, I am thankful for my friend, the modern day Maya Angelou, Catherine Ewing-Booker.

Introduction

Hey little broken wing butterfly. I have sat in your shoes in more ways than one. Let this book help you get through everything that you have been going thru. I believe God has called me to speak to those children who are hurting in silence. My words of encouragement will help your wing heal and be able to fly again. I wrote this book to inspire you in so many ways. The reason why I can fly my wings again is because God sent amazing people to help shape me. These people helped me fly again thru being a mentor, mother figure, and friend. He even used ones in my life that hurt me.

"All things work together for those that love Jesus." Roman 8:28 NIV.

I love him. I want to empower you and tell you that you are more than a conqueror. Even when you lost, you won. You might ask, "How did I win when all I see and feel is failure?" Everything in our life is for learning and growth.

I know what it feels like to be rejected. This means when one is not accepted or no one invites you to fun places. I know how it feels to lose a loved one. My mother passed away when I was ten years old. I know what it feels like to have a hole in your heart because you want that person to come back. This is called grieving. In all my pain that I experienced God had a plan. I feel like part of the plan is to speak to broken wing butterflies like yourself in order to help you fly again with confidence. I hope this book helps you to search for the gifts and callings that are already within you. Pick your head up. You are so loved and special. Fly butterfly, fly.

Love always,
Catherine Ewing-Booker

Butterfly Life Cycle

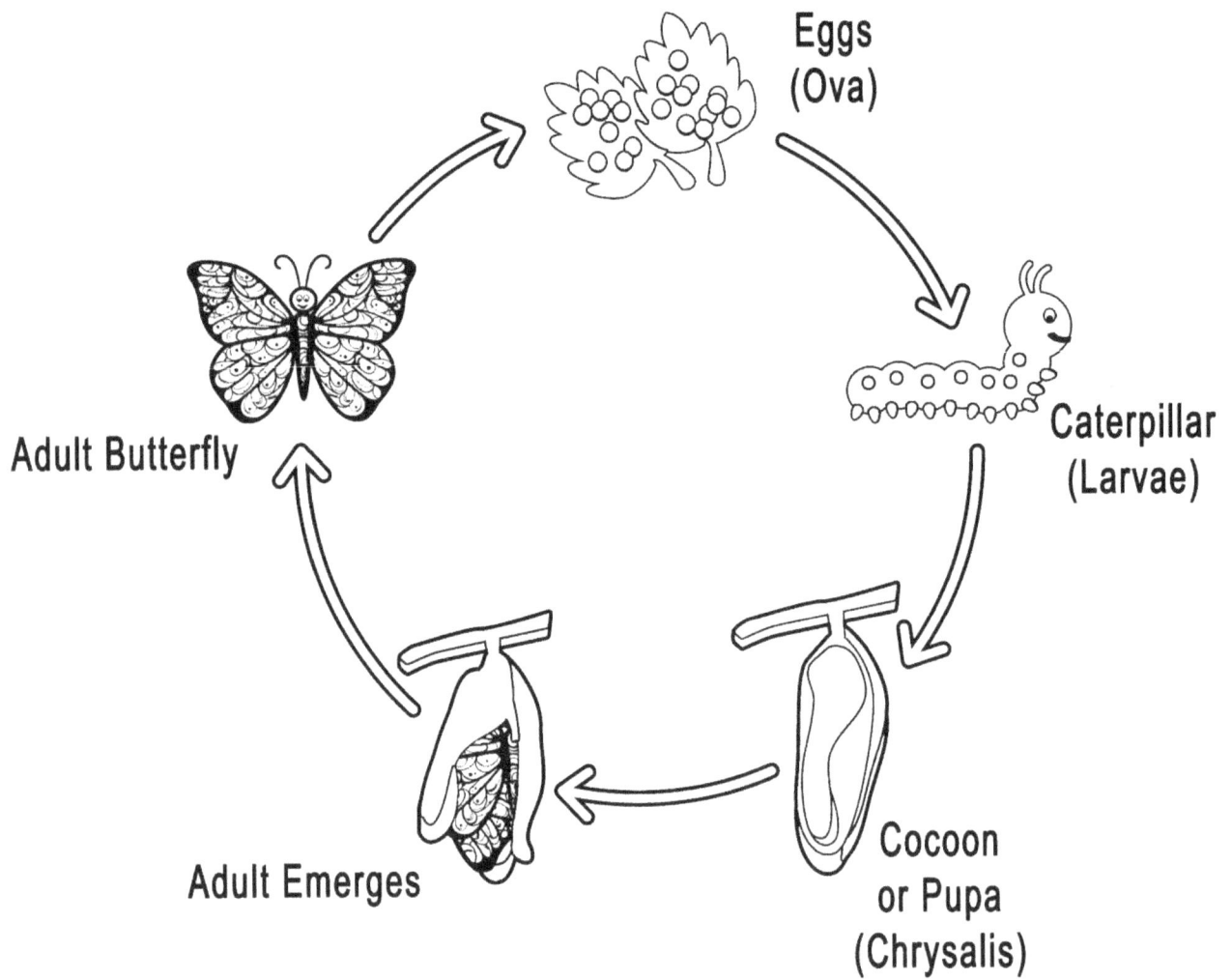

Eggs
(Ova)

Caterpillar
(Larvae)

Cocoon
or Pupa
(Chrysalis)

Adult Emerges

Adult Butterfly

Table of Contents

Bright One

I praised you because I am fearfully and wonderfully made; your works are wonderfully, I know that full well. Psalms 139:14 NIV

"Have you looked in the mirror lately little butterfly? Do you not see your beautiful dots and stripes?" You're colorful and glittering like gold. "Are you afraid to look at what I see?" Hey young lady? Hey young man? I think you are only focusing on your wing that has been damaged from people labeling you a bully and a dummy; told by people who you admire that you will never be anything. The same people who called you ugly and made fun of you because of your short comings. Your self-image has been polluted with negativity. These cruel words spoken over your life do not define your identity. Your words have the power to shape your destiny.

Life is a paint brush and not all of the strokes are glamorous and eye catching. Yet, in the mess there is beauty. Train your eyes to see past your deficiencies.

Bright one, look into the mirror of your heart and know that other people's opinions of you do not matter. Open your ears to my positivity. Let me tell you what I see. I see a mended wing butterfly with beautiful dots and stripes. I see a smart, intelligent, gifted, educated, and uplifting role model. A leader too many: trustworthy, helpful, kind and determined. I speak life! You are joyful and outstanding, with the heart of a servant. You are unified by the loving arms of loved ones and teachers that want to see you grow and become the best you. You are that bright mended wing butterfly that aims high and is cultivated in purpose, with a future full of light. Let my words be a pen that is writing on your heart. A pen that writes the words, "You are worthy," bright one.

Broken Wing Butterfly

He heals the brokenhearted and binds up their wounds.
Psalm 147:3 NASB

Let me tell you about me. Listen, because my scars have a story. I used to be a butterfly with a broken wing. Life wasn't always easy for me. I didn't live in the best neighborhood and losing my mother as a little girl was the hardest thing. I was void of calling another women mommy. This reality broke me. I lived in a fatherless home with no one to call daddy. I was just a little girl searching for love and attention. I was even acting out to get it. This broken wing butterfly used to come to school feeling unloved, with no friends, low self-esteem, singled out, and bullied. I didn't believe I was pretty and was very confused in my identity. It took me a long time to build a relationship with beauty. I was a broken wing butterfly looking for anyone who cared to see my broken wing of sadness and emotion healed. "I'm only a child but does anyone believe what I feel is real; that my emotions and anger are real?" Sometimes I would say to myself, "Does anyone see me?""Does anyone feel my pain?" I just want you to know that even though I have a broken wing, I am I fearfully and wonderfully made. "Will my broken wing ever fly again?" I said, "Will my broken wing ever fly again?"

I look around and see how high the other butterflies are soaring. As I'm fluttering in the middle, I look amazed while saying, "I will soar higher than a kite one day." I believe because I hear a voice in my spirit that says,

"I can do all things through Him who gives me strength to achieve." Philippians 4:13 NIV.

So I ask myself again, "Can this broken wing fly again?" I said, "Can this broken wing fly again?" The answer is, "Yes"!

I give credit to my faith, my mentors, my clergy, and my teachers who mended my broken wing to fly again. It's nothing like having a personal champion rooting for you along the way. My childhood life started in the pits. It may have been my beginning, but I'm here standing to tell you that it wasn't my end. As I look you in your eyes bright one, know that you are a prized treasure. You are called! You are chosen to give back to the earth the intelligence that is embedded within you. School wasn't easy for me. I overcame a lot with a learning disability. I had the confidence to know that I could achieve. I stand before you today with my Associates, Bachelors and Masters Degrees. My hope is in knowing that I might have short comings and flaws, but one thing I know for sure is that I am called. I am called to pull out the gem that's buried deeply inside of you. Let my words be a shovel that is digging for positivity to arise.

I know what it feels like to lose someone close. I know what it feels like to be rejected and pushed away. I know what it feels like to have people not believe in who you are. You are a butterfly that will fly high out of disparity. You will fly high and complete what you are destined to achieve.

"Persecuted, but not abandoned; struck down, but not destroyed. 2nd Corinthians 4:9 NIV

You are more than a conqueror Romans 8:37 NIV.

I said you are more than a conqueror! In the present I see children, but I also see social workers, doctors, lawyers, teachers, clergy, musicians, soldiers and beyond in the future. I have been assigned to the mind of children; to plant seeds in the hearts of you little butterflies with broken wings. I'm here for the children who feel unloved, forgotten and rejected. I'm here for the children who love school even though it's really hard. I speak life to the broken wing butterfly. Stay with it; you will arrive at the appointed time.

I didn't get to say goodbye

"Precious in the sight of the Lord is the death of his saints."
Psalm116:15

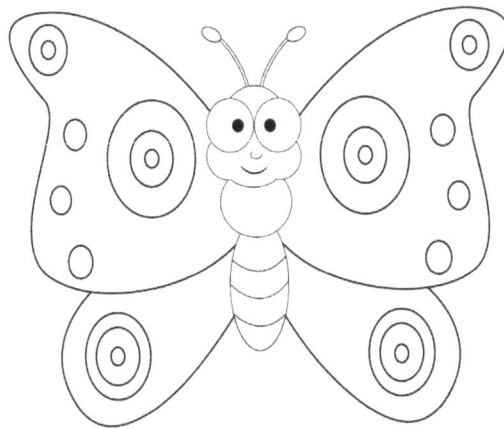

Sweet one, I didn't get to say goodbye. I left without telling you good night. I didn't read your favorite bed time story. If I were standing in front of you right now, I would tell you that I love you. We would have a heart connection through our hug, as your eyes stare into mine, while I thank God for my little sparrow.

Sweet one, I didn't get to say goodbye. Death came unannounced and now you are mourning your eyes out. Sweet one, let go of guilt. It's not your fault that I'm gone. A piece of me lives through you, so live on. Live and shine for me, while flourishing so others can see. You will have days you wish that I was with you, but always cherish my spirit and my love.

Sweet one I didn't get to say goodbye. Cherish the precious memories of my life. When you are blue, consider talking to the closet person to you. You don't have to struggle thru a loss alone; closure is on its journey looking for its home. Your emotions are real, but there comes a time when you must move on. Move on in my memories; move on in my love and let the pain of your loss fly away like a dove. We all have to leave this earth one day and my exit was thru sickness. I ran my race and kept my faith. Have hope, knowing I'm with my Savior and my King.

Sweet one, I didn't get to say goodbye. Please forgive me for the unannounced tears. My brain goes thru anguish, pain and fear. There's a constant voice that tell me to do self-harm and negative things to myself and sadly, this time sweet one, not thinking I gave in. A voice I hear daily tells me that I'm not good enough. I saw the world differently and wished people understood. Have you heard of mental illness? Yes, it carries a stigma that this world needs to erase. Mental illness is a reality like cancer that is starring the world in its face. Some people turn a blind eye and others advocate. Things that hurt my feelings dig in my thoughts like claws and I feel like I'm in sinking sand. Sweet one, I gave in to a deceiving voice. Sweet one BE A VOICE for THE VOICELESS; for those who suffer with mental illness such as depression, schizophrenia and PTSD.

Sweet one I didn't get to say goodbye but I'm saying it now. Goodbye sweet one, goodbye.

Love always

Warrior

"The Lord your God is with you, Mighty warrior who saves. He will take great delight in you; in his love he will no longer rebuke you, but will rejoice over you with singing." Zephaniah 3:17 NIV

You are beautiful; from the strand of your hair, to the way you are built. You are built with the heart of a warrior. Dance thru with that beat. Let them see you move to the north, south, west, and east. You are clothed with the full armor of God. You don't have to walk in defeat. The world is a box and God has given you more than what is in the box. Some children think they are missing out because they don't fit in the box. Child you are marked by Holy hands to stand out. You are marked by Holy hands to build, invent, transform and be the solution to a grieving world. Young butterfly you are not perfect. Yes, you made a mistake but quit living in regret and move forward in forgiveness of self. Love everything God has given you. Cherish your family and friends that God has assigned to your life. Meaningful relationships add to and prosper you. They challenge you to grow deeper. Iron sharpens iron, just as fire purifies the soul and burns away fear, insecurities, and doubt. When God was finished forming you He smiled and said, "This is my child with whom I am well pleased." Lord, give me Your eyes so I can see me inside out. I want to see my beauty. I want to accept myself and not be so judging. Give me your ears so I can hear truth and accept that I hear Your voice that says, "I love you." Give me Your mouth so I can boldly share the Gospel, so children my age can be saved. Give me Your heart so I can love people who hurt me. Give me Your legs so I can move with grace and mercy. With the tools You give me I want to build a castle of hope and speak life for those who need a place of refuge. Lord You built me with the heart of a warrior at such a young age.

I say yes to you and I will walk with you all the days of my life. Psalm 37:4-5

I will delight myself in You Lord, for You will give me the desires of my heart. I will commit my ways to the Lord. I will trust that whatever I need You will bring it to past. Little butterfly, the secret to success is to know that only what you do for Christ will last.

The voice of fear

So do not fear, for I am with you; do not be dismayed, for I am your God. I will strengthen you and help you; I will uphold you with my righteous right hand.
Isaiah 41:10 NIV

Fear sounds like a thunderstorm. It feels like heat melting your faith away. Fear has droopy eyes that are darkened with sadness. Its ears are dull to God's voice that says, "I'll give you the oil of gladness." Fear is a weapon of destruction against your destiny. I can say I always felt like I wasn't good enough. The world thru my eyes moved slower. It took longer to catch on. Other people opinions affected me, like hurricane Katrina did New Orleans. Words ripped me apart and flooded my heart until I drowned in low self-esteem. The seed of fear took root like an apple tree. So instead, I bear fruit of decay. Decay of people pleasing and trying to get people to like me. Fear became my identity and I couldn't even recognize myself. I became everything to everyone because I didn't want to lose my so call friends.

Fear gripped my potential, stole my passion, and rusted out my love to try news thing. My fear put me in a shell. My stomach was tight as my heart was rapidly pounding. My hands were sweating at the thought of just trying.

I hear a quiet still voice ask, "Do you have faith as small as a mustard seed?" Mathew 17:20 NIV Perfect love cast out fear 1 John 4:18 KJV

Trade in fear for courage, dreams, gifts and talents or they shall forever lie dormant. Fear is like feet stomping on your greatness. With Philippians 4:13 imprinted on your soul you can rise up and take over fear and say, "Greater is He that's inside me. I'm a child of the King."

Jesus wants it All

You shall love the Lord your God with all your heart, and with all your soul, and with all your strength, and with all your mind; and love your neighbor as yourself.

Luke 10:27

You might feel overlooked, but you are always discovered by God. You might seem dried up by sadness, but God is a water fountain that you can drink from. He wants it all; all of your affection. He doesn't want you to play tug of war with His love and things that you know you should not do. "What is your distraction?" "What is pulling at your mind?" "What is stealing your affection from Me?" The hole in your heart is so deep that everything you try to do to fill your emptiness will only make you feel incomplete. Hey little broken butterfly. You have been going to church all of your life, yet church is boring to you. You still have not received Jesus Christ. God says to you, "Taste and see that I am good. Try Me again; surrender your life.

Hey, little broken wing butterfly. You want to know Jesus, but you don't have a role model around you shining the light. You serve God how you see fit but God says He is sending you help, so don't let go of Him. He is your constant friend. He wants it all. He wants all the excuses and all the reasons why. He wants your devotion. "Will you trust Him with your deepest cry?" God is your strength. You are molded by the Master's hand; molded by the clay of His love. Trade in your low expectation for God's high expectation for your life. God sees you clean although you feel dirty. He sees you and nurtures your potential. He kisses you on the cheek and motivates you. He says, my daughter, my son, know that I love you without reason. I love you unconditionally. I love everything I created from scratch. In Me there is peace, freedom and love. Surrender your wants and desires in My heart and take hold of Me. I, the King, want it all today. Submit; draw close therefore to Me.

Resist the devil and he will flee. James 4:7

Come Home

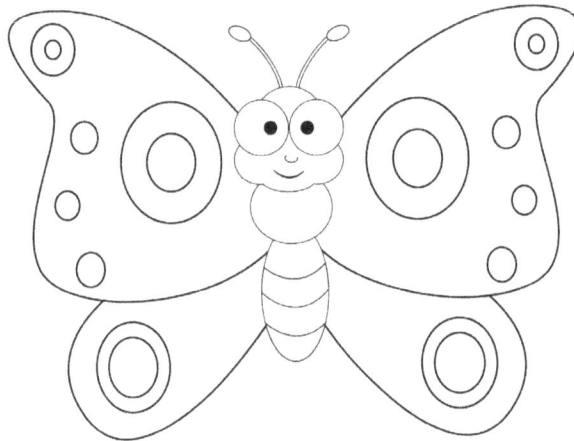

They said mommy did a bad thing. They said daddy made a huge mistake and this is why he was taken away. I just want my daddy; I just want my mommy back. I remember the night when I hid under my bed and watched them take my parents away. Those silver cuffs squeezed tightly around daddies and mommies wrists. I sat and cried, wanting them to take me as well. Daddy looked in my direction and said, "Baby I love you and I will be back soon."

I see my mom in that prison uniform crying uncontrollably. I'm sitting in her arms and she tells me that she will be coming home soon and to never forget that she loves me. As we depart, I ask my guardian, "What is that place called again?" They replied, "Prison."

My soul feels incomplete. It's on a journey trying to find home. My soul will not rest until it's freely hugging the neck of my parents like a tree.

This empty void keeps the inner self searching for connection. I feel like love is locked away in a box from me. I just want my loved ones to come home. I forgive you mommy for leaving. Dad, I no longer shall not hold a grudge against you, nor am I blaming myself any longer. I am free from anger and rejection.

I stare out the window blowing imaginary kisses your way in hope that it reaches your cheek. I pray for the day you come home and the imaginary kiss becomes real. The journey will then be over. Until that day comes, in heaven or on earth, I will wait for your return. I will live on until you come home.

Love, your Child

Don't give up

Be strong and courageous. Do not be afraid; do not be discouraged, for the Lord your God will be with you wherever you go. Joshua 1:9

Little butterfly don't give up. I can see the gloss in your eyes. You tried at it so many times and you feel like a failure. You studied so hard for that test and you still got an F. You practiced that dance routine and still got cut from the team. You tried and tried, yet rejection is surrounding you making you feel sad. Don't give up! Pick yourself up and try again. God has given us so many talents and gifts. Discover who you are. You have more than one talent. Little broken wing butterfly, I just want to encourage you with these dots and stripes and remind you of your beauty inside and out. I know you feel sad because all of your friends seem to excel, but if you excel in Christ, He will open up doors for you that no man can open. Please, don't give up! You have the heart of a warrior. You're more than a conqueror; put no confidence in the flesh, but allow your confidence to come from God.

You have the kindest, giving heart, yet you are always over looked by so many. Don't give up being a friend. You are needed to be a light. Little broken wing butterfly, I know it is hard to see God molding you in it all. Don't throw in the towel... You just can't give up now!

Dear Broken Wing Butterfly

The Lord is close to the broken hearted; he saved those who are crushed in spirit. Psalm 34:18 NIV

Dear Broken wing Butterfly,

I know you feel torn between the two. Your love feels divided because you have become the middle person. All of the custody battles, rejection and disappointments swallow you up like a tornado. Sometimes you feel like it's because of you. You have become a chess piece in a chess game. You became a sword in a war you didn't start. Your little brain is trying to figure out adult issues. You involuntarily have become the problem solver, the adult and referee in breaking up fights and arguments between your parents. Your focus is on the divorce so much that you are not doing well in school, experiencing loss of appetite, and loss of self. You are bombarded with emotions that you cannot handle properly just yet. Loneliness, anger, depression, and deep humiliation arise at any given moment. Tears stream uncontrollably down your face.

You are a broken wing butterfly trying to spread his or her wings to fly. You feel the hurt of your parent when it's your weekend to stay at one of their homes. You are drowning in pain and want to be rescued by your parents being married once again. You want to be rescued by their love for you. Reality hits and you must accept truth. Trust me; your life will be different.

Parent's response:

Son and daughter please forgive me for the pain that I have caused. I have been so selfish with my feelings that I have misplaced my affection and love for you. My baby, I cannot undo any damage that I have caused. Yet, I love you with all of me. I thank God for showing me my heart and my heart is you. I am broken because you are. Yes, broken but healed only to fly again. Let's start our journey as one so we can fly together.

The power of a smile

A time to be born and a time to die. A time to plant and a time to harvest. A time to kill and a time to heal. A time to tear down and a time to build up. A time to cry and a time to laugh.
Ecclesiastes 3:2-4 NIV

The most powerful thing we can do is cry and smile. It's like rain and thunder, yet out comes a rainbow. These are two actions that deep cleanse the soul. While we need our tears we also need our smile. The power of a smile is like drumsticks pounding on a drum set of positivity.

It releases out that feel good stuff called endorphins, serotonin and dopamine. They are all created by our powerful brain.

My child, rejoice and smile and pound on the drum of my heart loudly. I'll smile with you and dance hand in hand with happiness, while looking thru the eyes of joy.

Little one, do not be afraid to cry when you are hurt. Always keep a smile on your face even when others put you down. Love people who don't see you for who you are. Your smile helps you fight those negative thoughts of yourself. Be of good cheer. Be proud of who you are created to be. Know the power of a smile. Your smile is powerful and it's needed in your community, school, and family. So smile ear to ear and always be of good cheer.

Coloring Book

Broken Wing Butterfly

I AM
A BEAUTIFUL
BUTTERFLY

Philippians 4:13

I AM
AN OVERCOMING
BUTTERFLY

Philippians 4:13

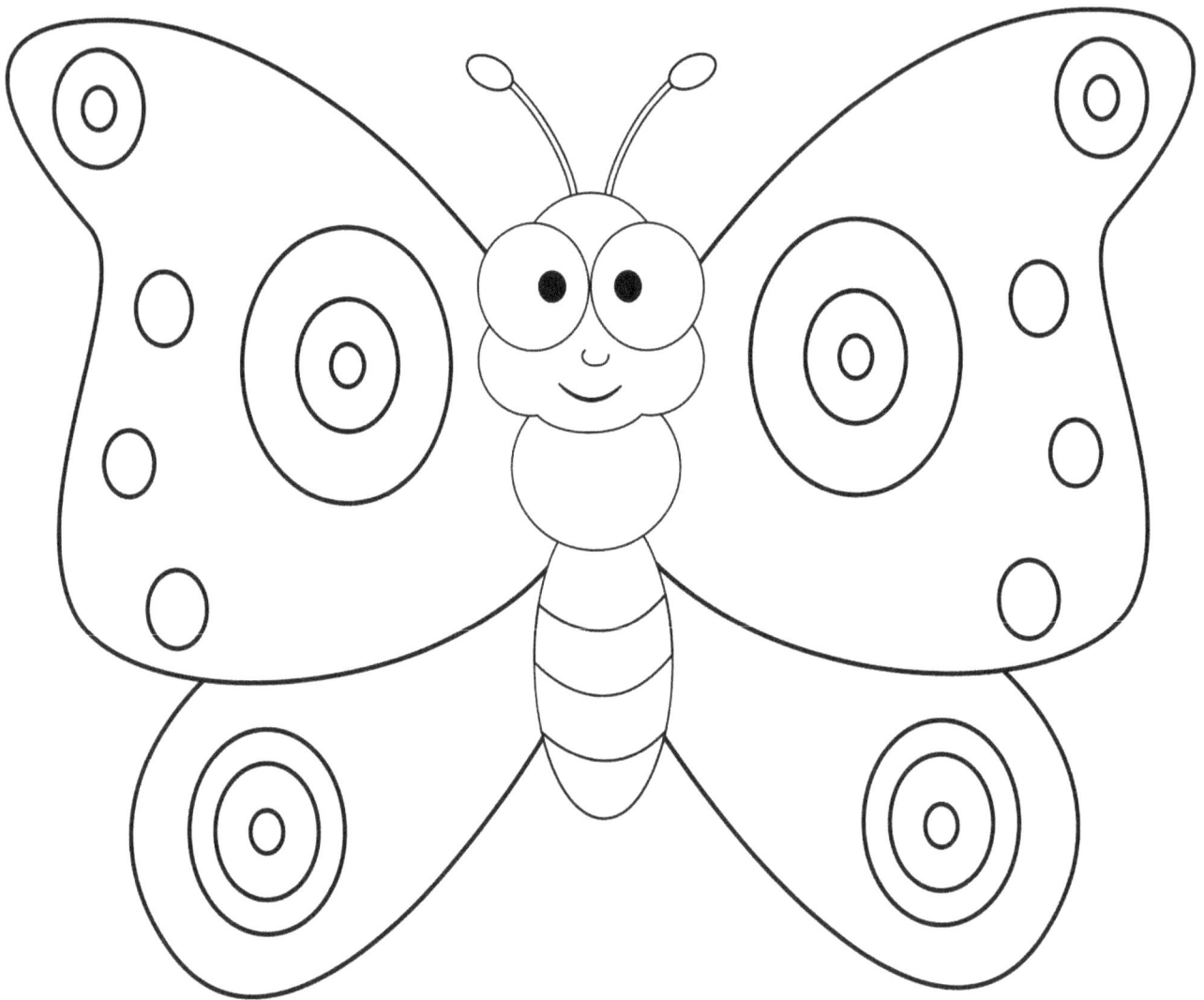

I AM
AN UNCONDITIONALLY LOVED
BUTTERFLY

Philippians 4:13

I AM
A STRONG
BUTTERFLY

Philippians 4:13

I AM
A BRAVE
BUTTERFLY

Philippians 4:13

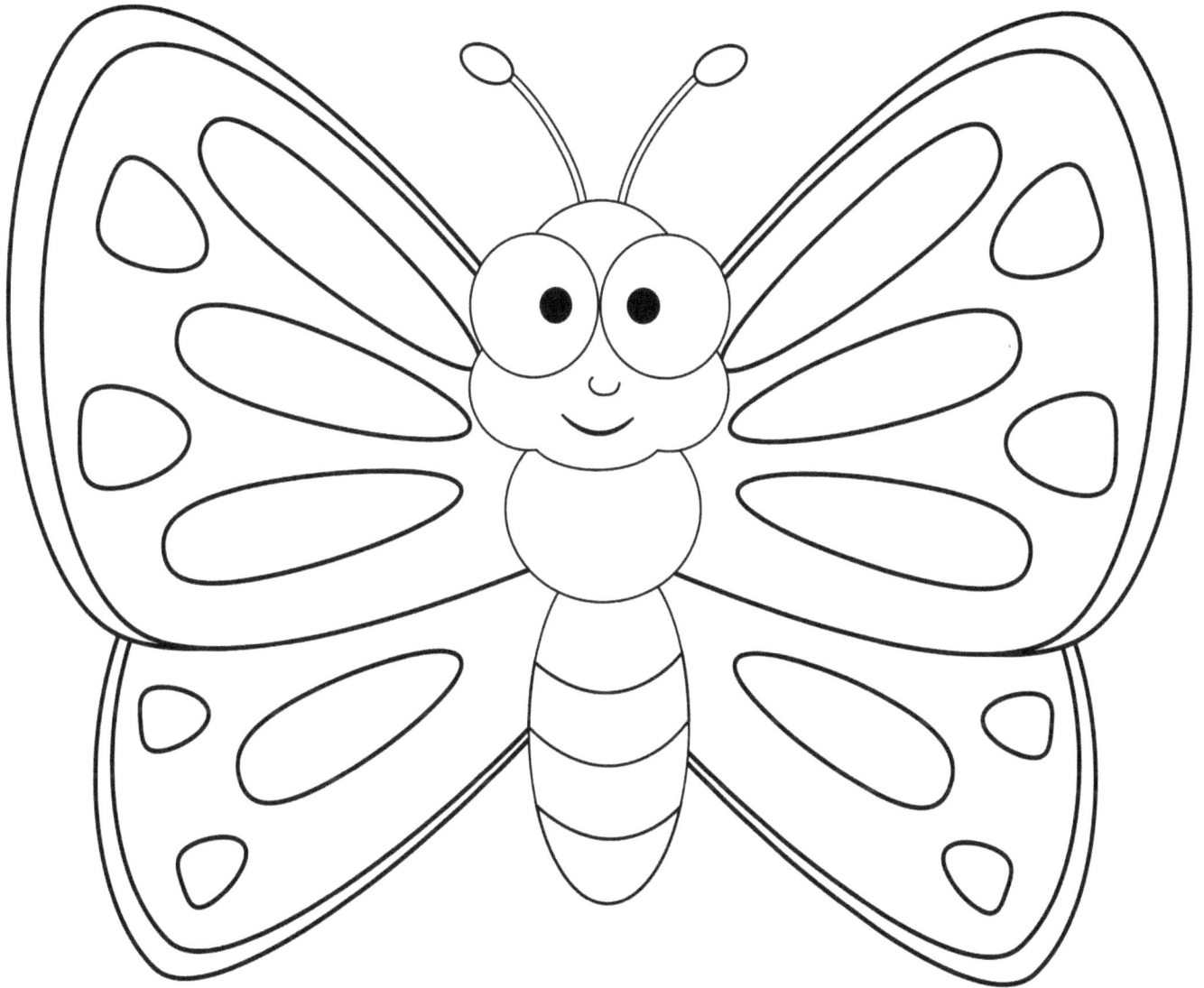

I AM
A CHOSEN
BUTTERFLY

Philippians 4:13

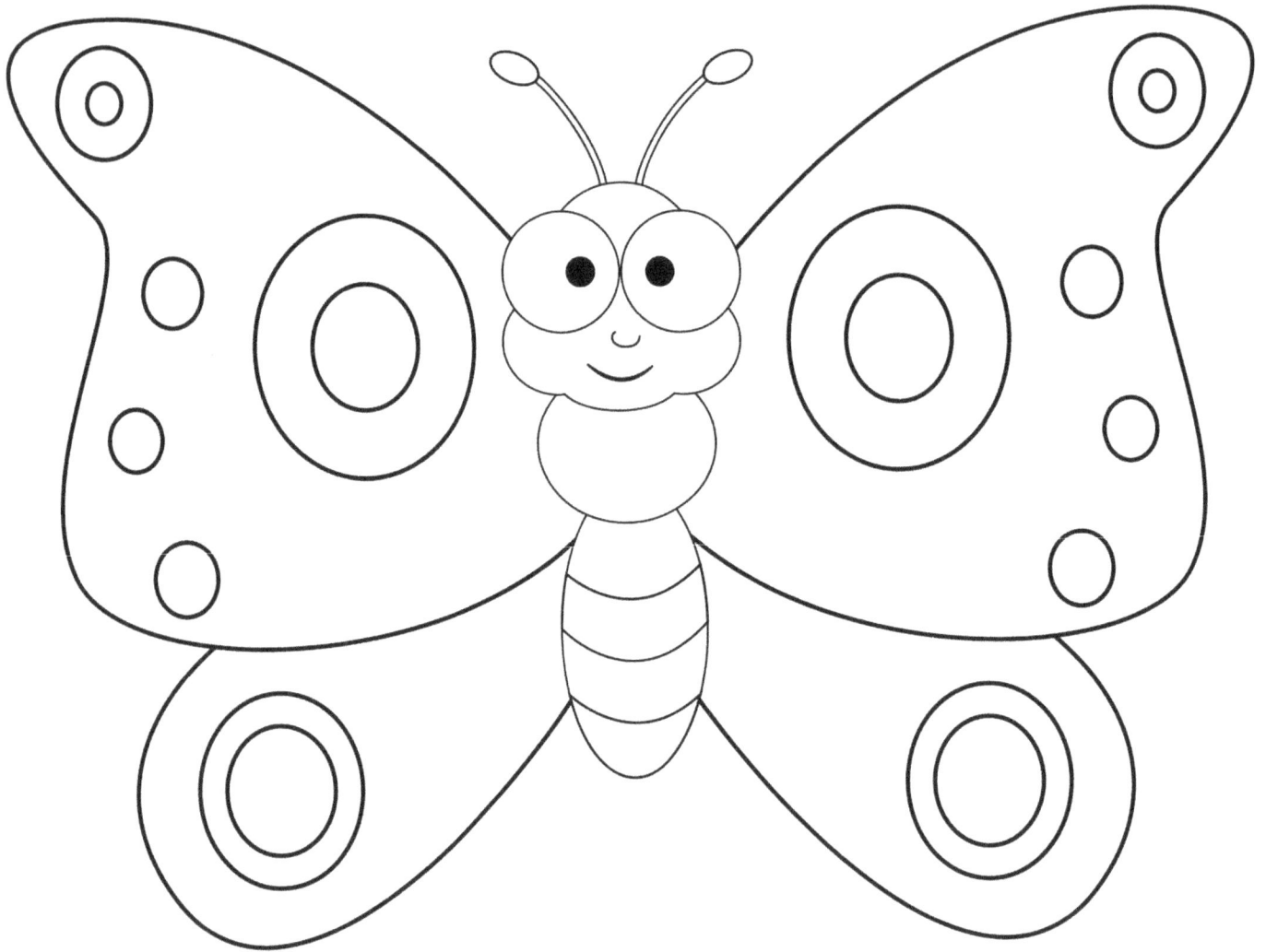

I AM
A PRAYING
BUTTERFLY

Philippians 4:13

I AM
A SMART
BUTTERFLY

Philippians 4:13

I AM
A CONFIDENT
BUTTERFLY

Philippians 4:13

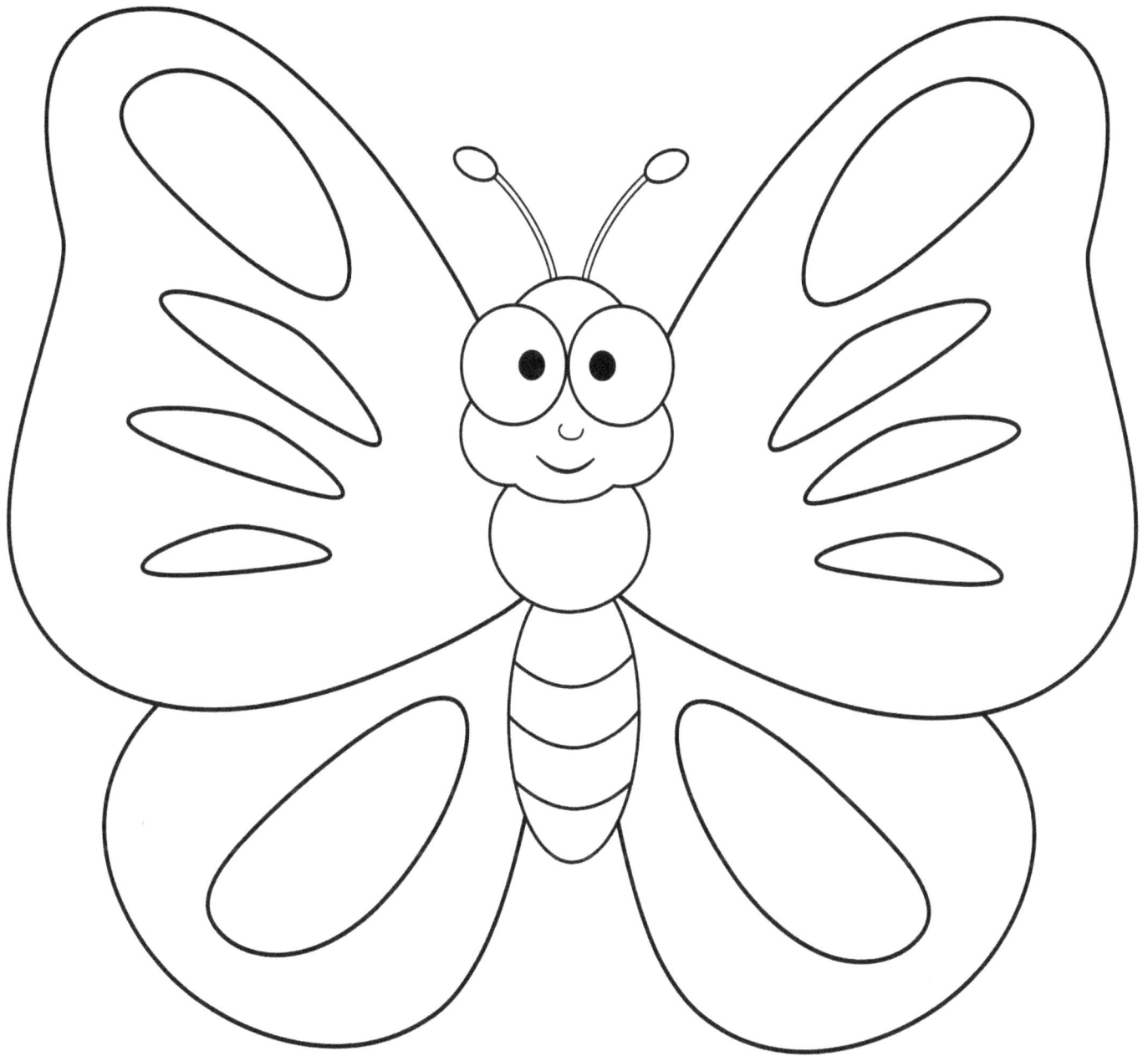

I AM
A JOYFUL
BUTTERFLY

Philippians 4:13

PURPOSE

Philippians 4:13

CARING

Philippians 4:13

SMART

Philippians 4:13

JOYFUL

Philippians 4:13

CONFIDENT

Philippians 4:13

DESTINY

Philippians 4:13

LOVED

Philippians 4:13

POWERFUL

Philippians 4:13

STRONG

Philippians 4:13

SAFE

Philippians 4:13

BRAVE

Philippians 4:13

CHOSEN

Philippians 4:13

OVER COMER

Philippians 4:13

About the Author

Catherine Ewing-Booker is a native from Milwaukee, Wisconsin. At the age of nine she relocated to Indianapolis, Indiana and lived there until graduating junior College. She currently resides in Evansville, Indiana. She is single and finds it a blessing to maximize her singleness being used and stretched by God. Catherine has an Associate Degree from Vincennes University and a Bachelor and Masters of Social Work Degree from the University of Southern Indiana. She is currently working as a Therapist at a community agency. She is a devoted person who loves Jesus Christ. She is a member of The Rock Global Outreach Ministries under the direction of Pastor Cameron Jones and Lady Tamera Jones.

In 2015, She published her first Non fiction novel titled "*Battle Axe For Emotional Healing.*" Her book is filled with power and solutions to overcoming injured emotions and restoration. She believes God's people are a weapon of war in His hand to tearing Satan's Kingdom down. This book can be purchased on Amazon.com

Catherine is very involved in her community through the African American Museum Soul Writers' Guild. She also loves ministering at women conferences, and community functions.

Catherine is a spoken word artist that loves presenting her works at different venues. She loves evangelizing those who are lost, especially children and young adults. She is very passionate about stirring the gifts in every child or young adult who crosses her path. In her free time she loves spending time with friends and family. She enjoys traveling, shopping, reading and growing in Jesus Christ.

You can connect with her on Facebook @Catherine Ewing-Booker and on Instagram at BattleAxe poet

Contact Catherine Ewing-Booker at catherine323270@gmail.com

BATTLEAXE & BUTTERFLY
MINISTRIES

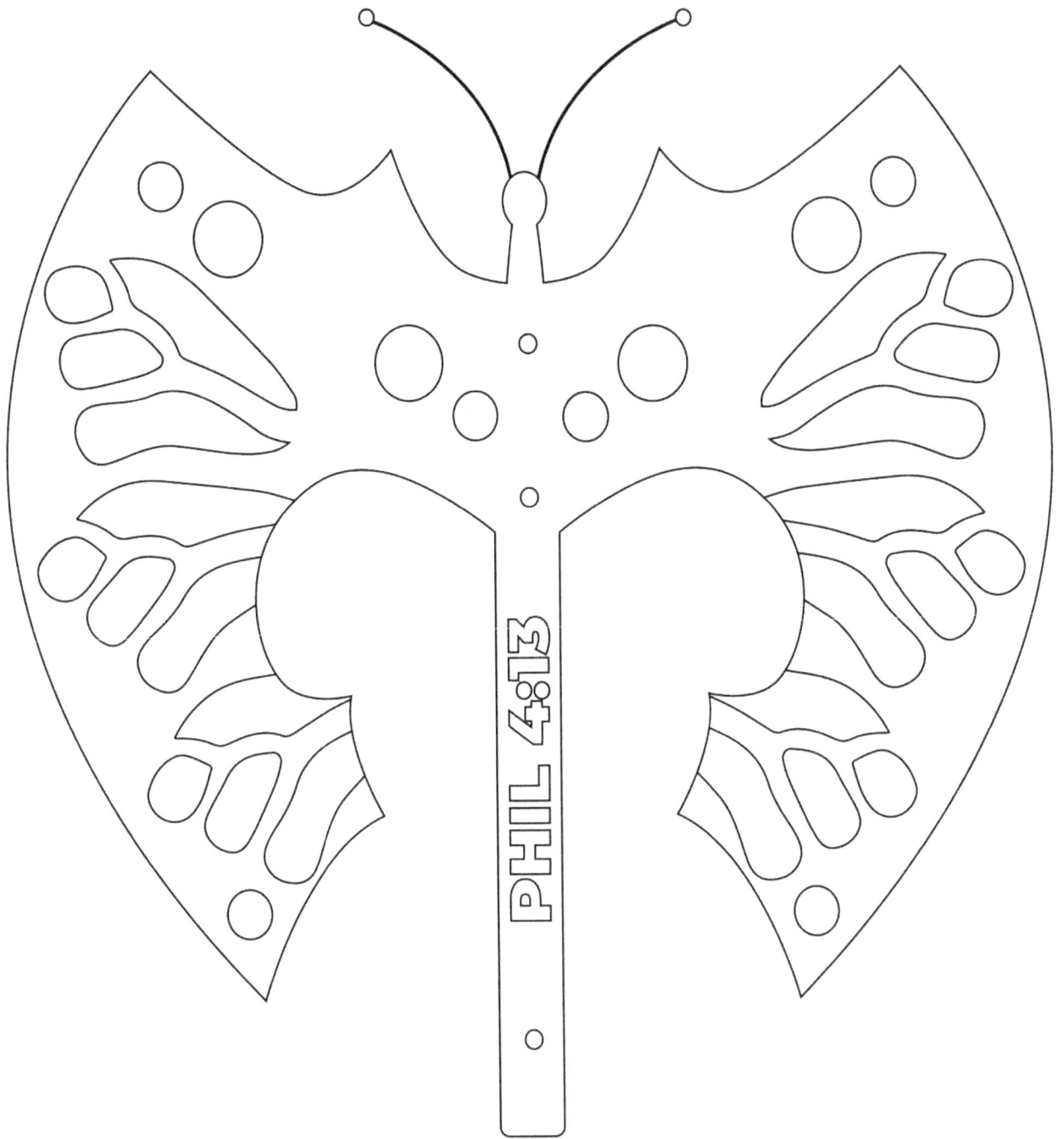

PHIL 4:13

BATTLEAXE&BUTTERFLY

MINISTRIES

www.ingramcontent.com/pod-product-compliance
Lightning Source LLC
Chambersburg PA
CBHW081546040426
42448CB00015B/3238